Angles of Separation

Angles of Separation
Copyright © 2014 Judith Skillman
Paperback ISBN: 978-0-9840352-9-8

All rights reserved: except for the purpose of quoting brief passages for review, no part of this book may be reproduced or transmitted in any form or by any means, electronic or mechanical, including photocopying, recording, or by any information storage and retrieval system, without permission in writing from the publisher.

Cover art: Edvard Munch: Separation 1896
              Oil on canvas
              96.5 x 127 cm
              Munch Museum, Oslo
              MM M 24 (Woll M 393)
              © Munch Museum / Munch-Ellingsen Group
                  ARS, New York 2014
              Photo © Munch Museum

Cover design: Steven Asmussen
Design & Layout: Steven Asmussen

Glass Lyre Press, LLC.
P.O. Box 2693
Glenview, IL 60026

www.GlassLyrePress.com

Angles of Separation

Judith Skillman

for Drew Skillman—

       his bivouacs

Acknowledgements

Thanks to these journals, where the following poems first appeared, some in slightly different versions:

"Rehearsing the Past," *Amethyst Arsenic*

"A Sliver of Heat," *Tampa Review*

"Nabokov's Notecards," *Portland Review*

"Canary," *Off the Coast*

"The Coyote Returns," "The Water Lily," *Pirene's Fountain*

"Concertina Wire," "The Sifting," *Conversations Across Borders (CAB), Centrum Foundation*

"Elusive Mysteries," *Midwest Quarterly Review*

"Seasonal Affective Disorder," "Shingles," *Journal of the American Medical Association (JAMA)*

"Estrangement," "Disgust," "Nobility," *J Journal*

"Somewhere the Sickle," "Umbel," "Trill," *Tar River Poetry*

"Angle of Separation," *Prairie Schooner*

"Graos," *Agave Magazine*

"A Glutton for Punishment," *Cimarron Review*

"Pincushion," *Iconoclast*

"A Brittle Seam," *The Aurorean*

"Such a Long Life," *Comstock Review*

"Cause and Effect," *The Mom Egg*

"Steller's Sea Cow," *Athenaeum; Best Indie Verse of New England*

"Watercress," *Cascadia Review*

"Infection," *Stickman Review*

"High-Strung" *American Literary Review*

"Wind," *Barnwood*

"If Miranda," *Blue Lyra Review*

"Blue Bells," *Message in a Bottle*

"Eating Tongue," "Like Little Mouths Drinking From," *Hamilton Stone Review*

"The Water Lily" also appears in the anthology *First Water*, Glass Lyre Press.

"Advancing Colors" and "Beating a Dead Horse," appear in the *Crab Creek Review 30th Anniversary Anthology*

My gratitude to my colleagues in poetry and the arts, who have encouraged my efforts and edited work over the years: Christianne Balk, Irene Bloom, Erika Carter, Pamela Gross, Pat Hurshell, Carol Ruth Kelly, Tina Kelley, Susan Lane, Anne Pitkin, Eileen Walsh Duncan, Joannie Stangeland, Mary Ellen Talley, and Lillo Way.

Thanks also to those teachers who have critiqued my work and helped me immeasurably, including Beth Bentley, Linda Bierds, Ann Darr, Madeline DeFrees, Jana Harris, Rod Jellema, David Wagoner, and Reed Whittemore.

Contents

1

The Front	17
Rehearsing the Past	18
A Sliver of Heat	19
The Deeps	20
Nabokov's Notecards	21
Canary	22
Prospero's Lagoon	23
The Coyote Returns	24
Umbel	25
Concertina Wire	26
The Sifting	27
Elusive Mysteries	28
Seasonal Affective Disorder	29

2

Trill	33
Estrangement	34
Beating a Dead Horse	35
Angle of Separation	36
Lengua	37
Pincushion	39
Thrum and Goad	40
A Brittle Seam	43
A Glutton for Punishment	44
Cause and Effect	45
Steller's Sea Cow	46
The Hand of Sky	48
Advancing Colors	49

3

Infection	55
Somewhere the Sickle	56
Grasshoppers	57
Leavings	59
Watercress	60
Disgust	61
Eating Tongue	62
Shingles	63
Paganini's Pinky	64
High-Strung	65
Such a Long Life	67
Starlings	68
Peel and Peel	69

4

Wind	73
My Pocket Gopher	74
Graos	76
Nobility	79
Spare	81
Bluebells	82
Walking the Spit	84
The Water Lily	86
If Miranda	87
Salt Marsh	88
Like Little Mouths Drinking From	90
Notes	92

"Who knows, when the word 'departure' is spoken
what kind of separation is at hand,
or of what that cock-crow is a token..."

Osip Mandelstam, *Tristia*

1

The Front

Sixty days without rain and you stand
in the yard, surrounded by black leaves,
the cough of an animal, and wind. You thought
summer would be enough but it wasn't
in the way nothing is ever enough.

No gift ends the wanting. Sixty dry days
in a wet place, even the bamboo creeping
back into itself, crisped and yellowed.
You the dowager, the widow, the soul
adventure-starved in Paradise.

When the purple cloud comes
from west southwest,
barometer bird tipped, swilling red liquid,
all you crave is the past. Nostalgia —
a number, a figure, a figment? What of girl-

hood didn't you get? Hooted at, whistled,
cat-called. Nick-named, exposed to, molested.
Toward what version of erotica
does bad weather beckon?
Day dreams? Fictions?

Sixty days as in the desert, and you
don't dare to abandon the mattress,
the jewelry, go back alone by plane
to all the ways chalk changes color
from pink to pale to night.

Rehearsing the Past

The slightly sweet aftermath
of some great finale—
its bitter moments, its betrayals.

Did it happen when they sprayed for sugar ants?
Put gabled vents in the attic?
Or one day when you woke submerged,

half in, half out of the bed.
Once sleep gave succor, stars wheeling zodiacal
at the zenith. Is it the chicken swooning

in the dirt, feathers splayed? The bale of cedar
dropped near the acreage?
You wander from list to list,

wanting to remove every vestige
of this remnant, yet it moves into you,
the farcical taste of a perfect day,

the deep night no lover dared to enter.
Even the topmost portion of dreams
skimmed from surface tension.

Yet your arms and legs still move
above weathered stones,
and on your feet, the water-bird's dexterous toes.

A Sliver of Heat

From the tar bubbles comes the Cyclops sun.
Come grasshoppers, sleeveless girls, yellows
imbued with the cries of childhood.

From the white birch trees' inset eyes
comes the burn-wound
of remembered infant-song.

There grasshoppers, strewn like paper clips,
flew up when foot falls disturbed dead calm.
Wings so light it seemed they were made of paper

appeared to glide in childhood.
At night the earth collided with comet hair
and you wanted to tip the Milky Way

into your parched throat, drain the cream
as well as all that curdled in argument
grown full with midday.

From the burn-wound of childhood,
its cicadas, second-hand cars, and oil siphoned
into engines where a storm came

and dropped its thunder-rain.
There the rainbow would swim grudgingly
in a little pool of grease.

The Deeps

We steer away from them.
There a sister or a cousin.
Here a tooth bobbing in a dream.
Possums plunder plums.
We sit at the helm with cocktails.
Steerage in the cargo bay.
A portion of amnesia.
The water plays at waves.
Perhaps it's only physics.
Concentric rings tell of fish.
We steer the craft as given.
Time in dry dock equals waste.
Perhaps sweet peas only grow at night,
when half-wild animals
pour from sewer grates.

Nabokov's Notecards

French panes where you waken—the room smaller,
the town foreign. The morning sun prismed,

cutting through one house to wing another.
The train whistle urgent, its butterflied

cars snaking as if through tunnels inside
other tunnels. The giftee can never

thank the giftor. Protagonist outside—
on leaving his prison-castle—blinks, dazed

by the escape route through green-blue waters.
You dream of counter-espionage, schisms.

Is it autumn come back to recommend
travel abroad, to dictate another

kind of aging, future's doppelgänger?
Double glass holds full moons: faint, feint, fainter.

Canary

On a perch in a cage
outside the shop, hanging
against a white-washed wall,
where a man who has seen
everything happen seven times
in one life
sits in a cheap chair
watching himself watching.
He will not call me *Senorita*
like the others, nor try
to sell me heavy necklaces
or articles of wood.
He will not sell the canary—
it preens and is well kept
enough to make its captivity
no more oppressive
than seven lives
lived consecutively
beneath the same sun
that tans the earth
and makes every bucket
of water heavier
and more precious,
when it spills with the sound
of a little, unpretentious song.

Prospero's Lagoon

No longer fenced in by the sea,
freshwater rushes out through pipes,
renders his island a narrow spit
on which he paces back and forth—
a tiger without its stripes.

Underwater the octopus' orange,
eightfold arms grasp rusted metal.
Ruins of a rowboat the last storm
washed in lie against driftwood,
the paint-peeling sky loses its color.

Here he can no longer conjure
women and wine, nor hear the slave
who held dark-tongued words.
He feels unlimbered. As if a palm
were stuck in his spine.

His head cracked like a coconut
last time he took a nap.
How'd he end up north
of the equator, so far
from where he began,

in youth, to tell stories of enchantment
and erotica, eons before the word *erosion?*

The Coyote Returns

The coyote returns from his day of foraging
in the suburbs. At dusk his coat, too yellow
to be a dog's, barely hides his ribs.

He's left a bone chewed to the marrow,
a few fish scales, a trace of gull blood.
Very little escapes the coyote.

His wariness long ago became symbolic,
key to the kingdom called hunger.
The coyote is like an intellectual

deprived of books, a Bohemian
without clothes or Polkas. When Venus shines
and darkness is full-bred, nothing

will keep this animal's prey alive—
nothing keep earth's grasses from matting
beneath the weight of so much sleeplessness.

With each howl thrown into the tone deaf heavens
what boomerangs back is a scale, chords of thirds
slapped like cards upon the table its cousin

sleeps beneath, dozing the dream of running.

Umbel

Framework of wild carrot,
cluster of stars,
obsolete sunshade,
diminutive of autumn

harbor us now
as we wander
into darkness—
far from the sun,
its ray and disc.

Inside out
umbrella, keep us
in this winter
and from straying

toward those others
where the snow-berried
grandmother
feathers a nest
for the mole.

Concertina Wire

You could look through the length of its doubled spiral.
Jump over its span into the vacant lot beyond.

It's no man's land—a contested territory—you long for.
To hitch your heart to a cause, to parachute

into that place neither side wishes to openly move on.
The hitch: horse apples ooze white latex sap.

Cows can be kept from falling into the canal by Osage orange.
Learn to care for an odor reminiscent of oranges,

to covet ugly heads—male and female, spherical but bumpy.
Call it sadness, these few cars rusting farther away than the past.

A '58 Chevy: orange sedan raising heaven's chrome wings.
What war, this bright season? Borne in whose cold fist?

Nothing to steal but the music booming from *Scott's Dairy Queen*.
Two boys with their father, bike-settled helmets.

Two brothers eating ice cream cones, tall and fluted.
The father tattooed everywhere his clothes end.

Almost you remember, though you weren't
yet born, Dannert wire, invented by the Germans.

A heavy ring that concertina'd out into ten-yard lengths.
If it hurts it must be entangled. Certain go-tos:

chronic illness, inbred laziness, and an especial varietal:
that pain born of summer. Wind wound into every kind of tree

and no money in any leaf, not even a dollar to wave a flag at.
Some days you think you were born in order to be torn apart.

The Sifting

Through the long hours of afternoon,
the torture of opera wedded to scents
of rising bread, a river of cardamom
merging with poppy seeds—this was the art
of childhood, not to be mastered, rather,
conquered by. All through the long hours
of an afternoon punctuated
by swipes of viola bow and their
attendant flats, always in residence
in the house of my parents, humbled
but not poor, its windows tinted by rain
sun, or snow, a house immoderately
fond of its yard, a yard gone spindly
with saplings in whose arches ballerinas
twirled, jetéd, and pirouetted come evening,
when droplets, flakes, or hail from Thor
fell, and thunder.

Elusive Mysteries

Again she is gone, Kore,
the maiden who held
a sheaf of wheat in her hand,
a flower. Cold fogs the yard,
the dog barks at hoarfrost.

Once more she has been abducted—
how cold she must be, beneath
the earth, shivering, her room
so small it could be a grave.
How many seeds will she eat?

And yet I remember her
singing, empty-handed, playing
at being pretty. I remember
the feathers in her hair,
how soft the green trellises

of trees knitting themselves
into willows above her head.
As if it were yesterday
I recall the sound of her name
in so many languages.

All the mothers calling, searching
their cellars, looking for stairs
down into the earth,
and she already complicit
with the underworld.

She the go-between for a hare,
a golden dog, a sick woman
on a thin mattress,
and twin owls whose yellow eyes
hold their prey in dilated pupils.

Seasonal Affective Disorder

Outside, birds on oiled wings
cross a sky barge-colored, stale.
The old man's become different

than himself. He casts his net
for arguments, lies listless
on a sofa covered in bright flowers

she selected. Their stems
prickle his side. Her voice—
not again—in the background—

going on about this or that.
Snow plies the streets of New York.
The borough's no longer navigable,

as his thoughts begin to vie
with memory, and, again, her hand
gestures, as if it were a signet

he could follow or understand.
The book *Judge and Jury*, back broken,
fans its pages on the coffee table.

He's halfway through. A lost,
last territory still left to conquer,
and winter just beginning its reign.

2

Trill

Ring-necked dove
>set
at the topmost branch.

The itch,
the summer
>of swollen heat
saying *snapdragon*
>>*snapdragon.*

Estrangement

In winter an iced sky lies inside
and alongside the body. Long nights
sleepless, punctuated by sleet.

Age harrows us. We unwind
slowly, our skin thins. The milk film
scans, with its good eye, that past

gone retrograde, left spinning
despite its lack of stars and moon.
In winter we sleep alone. The house

with two stories, its emptied rooms
singular as a waking dream,
or the city seven hours south of Paris

called *L'Age*. A town so small its church
held only a few pews. A man
without a job, a woman without

her health. Let the chalk sky
go on writing what it knows best:
scrawled winds of another front.

Like the second century martyr Perpetua,
coming now into the arena
to be mauled by lion, hyena, and laughter.

Beating a Dead Horse

I pull it up from the well, using a system of levers.

It weighs two tons.

Finally we are finished with this, I say, and begin the flogging.

Over and over I hit leathered skin tinged with black waters.

I slap hard, the good swarm of bees in my arm, Furies I named the horse after.

The beast opens one eye.

I am only beginning to be dead, the eye says, white full of infection, ready to turn.

The day half over, and the seasons I must walk carrying the horse—this betrayer, this Judas—there may be five left.

Five to go, I say, whipping out entrails, embalming the animal.

Ready to be buried? I spit into dust.

A few flies enter my mouth and I swallow them like hosts.

Angle of Separation

The blue trees
of winter
stand at intervals
with naked branches.

Even when the sun touches
them like the third
circle in the archer's
target, their burnt
cherry twigs hardly flinch.

A train passes
in the distance,
carrying its cargo
of smokers in black jackets.

How seldom,
the moments when
anguish lets go
its hold on the little
chlorine pool,
the trellised courtyard.

And it must be so
for me as well.

My break with the past
will be taken customarily,
as a crust of bread
or a few flakes of snow
falling surreptitiously
into my mouth
to sever my tongue.

Lengua

They called it, after it was boiled
and skinned, the pink and gray moss
cut like a banner from the rest.

Because they—happy, healthy, ran to the plank—
a wooden table like the talking
dreams I had the night before,

I ate the pick-thin pieces
on my straw plate. Not too hot
nor cold: Mediterranean, room-temperature.

There's a certain conceit
in holding a fork so small. Once
the fingers touch the lips,

a bit of grace comes into the body.
Sometimes heavily seasoned.
Other times with mushrooms

and watercress picked just hours
earlier from the creek—like a salad
perched atop an island.

A woman is the same in another language,
and also a man with his knife.
This organ of many names,

a bit tough, harsh with the Polish horseradish,
I could say it never melted.
But that would be facile—for a complex

problem such as eating a cow's tongue
far more argument is required,
discretion, a pinch of salt,

a salt lick or a lame horse,
and all the ways lies stick
like feathers to the back of the throat.

Pincushion

I have been wounded by my occupation—
to hold these points, not to complain.
Verbs are my garden.

You see an antique, a runner
sending out its smaller version.
You laugh as if it's a joke to be pregnant

with meaning. I have no answer
for the domestic hunger—yours—
or the leaf motif above a muse

who will turn toward and away from
you in spring. If I am anthropomorphic
with desire for the human, still I tend

your dresses and curtains. My stuffing
keeps the barbs of your jokes.
You slander the other, you lecture

the husband rocking on his sofa,
the self growing old inside your breast.
Tell me—how far off the path does it grow—

the single strawberry, that wild orphan
of dream—a flesh nightmare repeated
night after night after night.

Thrum and Goad

Just as, summer nights
in the east
humidity prevailed,
    here heat presides
over the torturous powerlessness
    of childhood.

The insects take up their songs.
Lime-green katydids,
    grouse-colored crickets
        in stridulation.

Katydid, katydid
    ch ch ch
ch ch ch
against the lightning-
    cathedraled sky.

*

Working steadily higher
in brush near the Yakima River
whose water gave the town
its name—
    Swift Water—
        Cle Elum,
comes the train.

A whistled warning,
a threading of tracks
part seconds,
    part wood.

Do you hear awe before the silence?

Or night and nothing, rest note
      of head on pillow.

*

Who are we that we
might journey away
      from linked pasts?

Your anger runs its course
      pitched between the *April Shuffler*
and thunder, heat-blasts
      coming as claps.

*

      For the chirper,
calling occurs in waves and appears to be contagious.

Your older brothers knew exactly
      how to exert pressure,
         with what force.

The locusts, the crickets play their parts
      on blue-gray stones
in this mis en scene.

*

What shades are these
      whispering like locusts
in black oaks?
How many years between plagues?

I have touched luck,

       found clover, four-leafed,
in the spine of a book.

I hunger for what is true
       in all the teasing,
for one word—
onomatopoeia—
       that sounds like what
it represents.

*

Stem of a sapling,
       brown-colored conehead,
endear yourself
       with a whistle, a word, anything
       unbarbed.

I yearn for the cessation of wing beats.
For what floats noiselessly in still
       waters—
fossil of the stick that bridges
       victimhood. The crown
won by not taking a stand.

A Brittle Seam

Already the train whistle,
the frozen light. Pampas grass raising
its blonde flag, roofs steaming, trees dripping.
The shortest day—a droplet, a prism
of light creeping through fence slats.
Thin birds, a cornucopia feasting on zero
in the garden. Where the horizon lies
close to the lake, there will be steam,
as if I were still bleeding into her.
Impressionistic—these drops melting through clear air
to land on half-frozen grounds. The patio table
sealed with plastic cloth. Each leafless branch
rising vertical, diagonals spiked as with barbed wire.
The pots green with moss, the last hardy fuchsia bloom
I coveted through fall gone, its little bells of crimson,
its pagoda where the hanging lantern
lit up her little kicks half a winter
in the last hard pregnancy, in amniotic fluid.

A Glutton for Punishment

I swim up from my dreams. Already it's late, almost noon, and the cooks have detailed huge feasts for the unknown guest, to be fêted or punished—which is which? The great sky, white as an eye, the yard filled with cherry petal snow—how will I know what season it is? The gnats have moved into my eyes where they float up and down on see-saws, as in the play yard. The children, removed to other rooms, invent their own children. As for me, I have forgotten how it's done. In a bush outside the aging hole of a window a great-winged moth or a small exotic bird shivers. The cooks go on with their preparations, and I remember dreaming of food all night. Aha, I think, it's the scent of yeast and crème brûlée rising in the kitchen. But when I return to the kitchen, nothing lives there, nothing fills the saucepans fitted like Russian dolls one inside the one inside the other.

Cause and Effect

If I wind up my hand,
it will play a song. No, listen,
if I get down on my knees
and beg, if underneath the ferns
there are insects with voices,
some big-celled argument
comes true. Behind the grimace
in cold spring the word romance,
if I wind up my hand.
A certain cruelty thrives.
Beneath the forest floor spongy
with mushroom-laced spoors.
After the canopy of the trees
beings with extra shadows
copy themselves onto trunks
and water. The comb holds
our sex, and the pattern of violence
makes and mocks us.
If I wind up my hand,
it will play the tune
you wanted to hear.

Steller's Sea Cow
with remarks by Georg Steller

I saw the last one die.
Stout forelimbs slack against sand,
the head too small,
the skin black and thick...

like the bark of an old oak.

If that was it, I doubt myself.
At dinner last night, I picked up a soup spoon
and a knife and began cutting away
at sirloin.

It has no teeth but only two flat white bones—

Subcutaneous oil burns scentless.
I wake to dreams
of bleeding-hearts, rakes, and passenger pigeons,
their feet wrapped in fortune cookies.

The animal never comes out on shore...

I saw it come out of hiding to be part of Kipling's story,
"The White Seal." *H. gigas*,
killed by men for being tame
as much as fat—

one (tooth) above, the other below.

The kelp vine nearby
bulbed and green, a tendril
of consciousness burning in its gut—
that longing for the herd.

...but always lives in the water.

Those last three decades,
they were like Eliot's mermaids,
buttery creatures who coveted
the urge to be beached.

The Hand of Sky

Wet curtains draped with birds,
the kind you want to touch
in an old theater, where, behind brocade,
the sheers come into play—
then poplin, chenille, another draped chintz.

Alacrity you can see through:
the water in sky, the sky in the water.
To touch the memory of clouds
passing overhead in shapes of farm animals,
when you lay on the hill, your back

molded to earth as if earth
would never betray you, pull you down
into its tar face. Wet and then dry,
your hands, the sky, its surface
where leaves swirl slowly as into syrup,

marginalized by the frame. The last wish
left from summer, moving purposelessly
in its small dervish born from a tumult
of air. Until finally the cold
comes to steal peach-blushed sunsets

and, with them, a language of backward words
spoken into a vacant space where, ages ago,
mother and daughter were one.
The leaves, the snow, the singleness
wherein a multitude of selves

become resigned to the only body.
Pampas stalks impinge upon every drama—
giant feathers of an Arabian princess
tended by her only master,
his gray flannel suit worn pale.

Advancing Colors

A poisonous sun.

*

Anything more than cream, crème—
a beige tinted with gold's false cousin,
a carmine. I recall she had the dot dreams.
She was afraid of wind.

*

Everything's infected with time—
the white tree in the distance,
its halo of flowers,
the dreams of money, & perpetrators.

*

The silence too, inside, where pain lies.
An epidemic reigns in spring.
Not the precious symbol of flower and leaf.

*

Burrow back into sleep.

*

Its sheer face broken like glass or water
by the struggle to wake—
left over right, the sinister eye, *la gauche et la droit*.

*

Curb language

& it will cry again in a different tongue.

*

A wire chair, a table
set with nihilism. Come greet the day
as it goes—light of early springtime
tickling the canopy
of each tree in the wetland.

*

Glowering cherry
with its head of flowering whites.

*

Stricture as structure.

*

All infected with time—
the onrushing annihilation of age,
idiom's cousins nipped in the bud.

*

The white tree in the distance,
is it a cherry? The questions breathe
in solitude, beget other queries—
how is your health?

*

A fur of flowers—myopia's blessing.

*

Repetitive dreams of money: how
when money's gone, each dollar
spent, the bankroll unwound
from its secret life of nakedness,
even green begs to be forgiven.

3

Infection

No, it is not like that brocade and silk
you remember in your mother's house.

Nor is it to be pitied or skulked away from,
as if it too had a choice as to where to live.

Rather the mucus-cyst of the moon
given freely to earth's residents by the sun.

If you make a wish on a star, be careful
of all the other stars clustered around that one.

Jealousy breeds envy, and, from greens,
yellows grow. It is not only fabrication.

Still we would have preferred other news.
If we come to visit you, pretend you are well.

In the event you have trouble understanding
what's been happening in your glands,

your lymph nodes, begin again as a child.
Sound things out. Refer to pain as *ouch*.

In order to live with boils, rashes, and hosts,
yes, you must become yourself. Parasitic.

Need those who most rebuke you. Crave
what you can't have, wear the hair shirt

to bed, and carry your sins on a chain
around your neck, especially the Christ,

whose exit, impeccable, from gangrenous
rags left in a tomb, mimics the butterfly.

Somewhere the Sickle

Still moves in the wake
  of its silver arc.
Have cornflowers dried,
  wedded to thistles?

I know we passed the man who cranked
  the old blade to one side.
Was it a dream—
  Model T parked in a thicket of lilacs?

As in an etching—
  the barrel prone, the man pulling
his grass hook towards himself.

Its whistling
  left to right, as long-bunched grasses
shook reedy heads, falling
  around his boots.

Somewhere the scythe
  supersedes the sickle,
its handle grim
  with premeditation.

Grasshoppers

Too light for earth, match heads
rising up at each step.
Too fast to catch, already broken.

Tokens and talismans of the East,
Brittle. Wildflowers will bloom
from Taylor Bridge all the way

to Lake Chelan next spring,
thanks to the fire chewing acres,
sparked by a welder.

Once grasshoppers, like fire,
enchanted children. Children were told
not to touch flames, and grasshoppers

leapt in hordes before their minions.
A symbol can't be captured,
the child fell, got up,

ran only forward, never back,
carrying her small green arms.
Too light, *ein sof,* for earth,

wildfires flickering in the east
where the sun will set, head first,
breech-birthed into Red Top Mountain.

If the hinged arms, the bent forms,
sang as well as leapt, then the child
flew, mischief flickering in her eyes.

Who hasn't thought of the dead
while following a path to the river?
Or fought change by standing

still? In every pocket of sky
an astral channel, a constellation
of the Kabbalah. In this story

the child sees ten lights shining
in ten vessels. All colors dance
inside her face. The welder stops,

removes thick glasses,
wipes sweat from his brow.
Match heads return to safety boxes

as the tens of thousands
continue toward the horizon,
becoming, in time,

a line of char, a smile
of *no thingness*: infinity
humming as with electricity.

Leavings

In back of the flat I planted
a finger. Worms came
to leaven the soil. A trill—
dada dada dada.
Away from the room,
in rain and early dusk,
I planted other oddments:
a cork bridge,
a fist. Though bound,
how those crossed fingers
longed to arch and touch.

Watercress

Gin clear, the stream, and the couple
walking it. Picking leaves with hollow stems
      for their pepper-tang.

When we grow rich with trout,
      we must dabble there.
Meanwhile I write to you
      not out of need
so much as the wish for engagement,
for clusters of mustard,
small white and green flowers.

Anguish is like that—
hydroponic, well-suited to its wet plastic sack,
      lasting a day or two at market.

When we, old and poor,
walk along train tracks, looking down,
      there will be the same waters
ventilated by chalks in the soil,
letting down from the spring.

In the meantime try not to bleed
      quite so much. The Talmud
has a word for this radish-like plant.

Reinvent the old as new, it still
      grows in a ditch like a fool,
a poisonous version in backwaters,
mapped by hand-like protuberances—
(how outlandish the body becomes)
      the same as entrapment.

Disgust

The whole world finally quiet
and all you feel is a bit of rust
in your veins. *C'est dégolas,*
they said, when they wanted
to convey the worst. No one
could explain it—a word
doesn't translate its disease.
You would cross the Atlantic
on a red eye for the scratchy,
unlined wool coat an aunt
bought you on a Paris street.
For breaded veal cutlets,
raw frog's legs and mussels
you force down your throat,
swallowing more *Beaujolais,*
smiling at the part: sixteen
and abroad with a violin
aka machine gun. So many men
to stop you on the street, ask
what's inside the hard-shell case.

Eating Tongue

Nights they served tongue were different, not in a secular holiday
way, rather as grown-ups who interrupted one another more than

listening to what was said. Who had the last word, who had the most
persuasive argument over money, which maid stole what from whom,

best maps for routes the AAA recommended on honeymoon trips to
    Niagara Falls.
The tongue was repugnant in and of itself, not on account of not praying

before dinner, or not knowing who Jesus was in fourth grade, nor because
electricity was dangerous to the physicist.

Cords arrayed this way and that, venom of snakes.
This tongue, as if borrowed from Gulliver, had veins sticking out

on the bottom, a swayback, an arching forward, and pink moss turning
gray toward the tip. The cow no one could not see stood placidly

at the table, black and white ovals milking the joke of a dining room.
Rather than passing out to avoid the inevitable,

picking around the peas and carrots and mashed potatoes, fork-painting
the pat of butter—instead of asking to be excused aka humiliated, the tines

picked up a small piece, the mouth opened, soldier teeth chewed muscle,
swallowed mechanically. Please remain the same as if this never
    happened,

those of you who never had the chance to eat with a family so inbred,
so solicitous, so guilty of what Lengua with sautéed mushrooms does to a
    tremulous ego.

Shingles

My body,
 their house.
Their raised welts,
 the overlapping siding.

As if a carpenter
 living inside my hip
works ceaselessly,
digging at synapses with his awl.

I am driven
in the fallen world
by whorls
 that tell me where
my nerves lie.

Once-pale skin
reddens, thickens,
 seeps yellow fluid.
Sealing my joints,
 their blistered hinges.

Devil's itch
 that festers
at questions
beyond good, evil.

Shall we be bitter
or resigned,
 the burnt skin
plucked at, as pain's
lyre, singing
at dawn?

Paganini's Pinky

Like a rodent's tail it trails the carriage: flesh-toned,
long enough to anchor the right hand in its death cast.

Engorged with pebbles, like the frog of a horse—sensitive,
callous-shod, poised to fable four octaves and double back for
          pizzicato.

Then again it's only a quirk of nature, a by-product, symptom
of Marfan's disease, syphilis, or speculation.

If mute, he'll enter the concert hall as pale as he is tall,
play the part of a witch's child, his back bowed by scoliosis.

The pinky dangles inside his skinny black braid.
The bridge anchors the fingerboard—an ornament gone gangrenous.

Four black horses run on stones beneath the moon.
A sinuous road carries this maestro who bangs around

inside his cage as all of him becomes loose, lax,
pliant enough to execute whatever romance requires.

High-Strung

I weave the night
from nothing in particular:
a rebellion against,
a trampling upon,
the instant before fight or flight.

Green blood in the culverts,
frogs high-jumping
from bank to medusa head—
an upended tree
slipped into the river by storm.
The end of days, where a man,
picnicking in a field fenced by poplars
loses his keys.

I am the metal detector
aimed at grass,
the potato bug curled like a fetus,
the slender branch
erupting from its swath
of blackberries and thorns,
stripped, excited by wind.

I am the green horse, the insomniac.
Always the same lesson,
studied and lost
like the man's keys,
the young woman
on hands and knees
searching a hectare for its purse.

When the moon's
just past full,
on the brink of autumn,
corn silk whispering
against leaves, I am the fist
and the money.

Go ahead, plant my feet.
The cliff falls away when you run
with your orange wings,
with the man on your back.
All you see below the ledge
can be taken like a pulse.

Such a Long Life
after Jack Gilbert

At first it is the salt-taste of bridges,
the strangeness of animals,
the orange horizon scrawled
by winter sunset. We take this lineage in,
and it gives us back our own, like Bluebloods
persecuted in a forest. We come to be afraid
of limned windows, the strangers
behind blinds, the streetlights haloed
by myopia, the past pulling all our fathers
into hunger's single crib. The more we stare
at the moon, the more we see its pockmarks
and pits, seas and valleys where once
the surface was undisturbed. In this
we are like the children we bear,
who give back their immortality
as if it were nothing more than a coin
to be thrown in a well after the one wish was made.
With little more than half a moon
and the rain-gnawed spit-misted sun,
we come of age in order to bear luster,
to beat our short arms
against the swath of blue-green that hovers
in the brevity between.

Starlings

Tonight they line bars of music—
the starlings gathered on wires like hundreds

of crowded sixteenth notes. It's that way
the world enters your eyes—too much beauty

and song ever to understand. The more
space you take up, the more they press

together on electric lines: the concerto
you bailed on, the instrument you dropped.

Each rounded breast holds feathers. And you
too tender to take the brush against skin—

it lights your nerves. Signals cross
when you talk to the man.

The starlings gather for nightfall,
know their own kind. Would rather sit a spell

beside traffic than become part of a lake
as large as a city. What kind of thoughts besiege

the conductor who faces your particular,
obsessive, sequestered orchestra?

How fast can you count? Will you name
this sonata after the moon or the sun?

Peel and Peel

Strips of bark curl away
from eucalyptus
like burnt paper.
The tree you climbed when young
you take shade from now.
Scent rustles, a grove
groans as trunks rub
against one another in wind.
The wood cabin
falls back into itself—
there the hired hands
slept in shifts between milkings.
Dream these silvered leaves
fall like birds, lie reddened
on the path, for you—
your scribble sap, your kind,
for whom the earth perished
in its middle age.

4

Wind

Like pain it came and left by halves
and now mostly it stays on,
a boarder too poor to leave.

Like cottonwood it coated scenes
of past lives, and now it breathes in
heady gusts of her, as chunks calve

from her ego the way a glacier loosens
its sides to water. Wind, like air,
is not like anything, she thinks.

Ivory sheers hang to blot
the sun's bright face close to solstice.
She didn't think she'd end up like this,

one of Macbeth's three witches
stirring words together, whispering
curses under her breath.

All tenses conspire.
Sun lights hearts of ivy, the yard
overgrown, as when desire

first departed on its thin-ribbed horse
for another land, and the door
slammed shut of its own accord.

My Pocket Gopher

It wasn't so bad before he began digging
his way in. We lived for years like the married,
avoided sensitive areas, knew
the taboos. His cheek pouches held memos
I wrote but couldn't send to the others.

Better than a shredder, more secure. He
only left my shirt late at night to work
the tunnels honeycombed under the house,
a system of branched openings sealed
tight with earthen plugs. At dawn he returned

to my shirt. His stripes matched the pinstripe
costume I selected from a closet
open year round, full of the same shirt
pronouncing its brand name on a tag sewn
right next to the bulge of his compact body.

I didn't mind the company, though
we both preferred to be alone, away
from our widespread families—the fresh soil
in mounds to advertise what would better
have been left unknown. Flower beds, lawns,

gardens—all fair game to the habits
of damage. I grew to love the familiar ritual
of his return, worried he'd be cropped
by legalities. In order to keep
the gopher safe I imagined we were a pair.

I managed my small orchard obsession-
style, never invaded members of my
own family with bait though God knows
they deserved it. Carrots, apples, lettuce—
none of these kept my gopher from eroding

the world I could see. It was the inner
place, those wires driven like probes in between
the confidence I projected like
poison: it was the inside the gopher
was after. As tenant of my body

how could I eradicate experiences
honed by dowels and diameters, set
like the two-pronged pincher or Macabee
trap, the choker-style box that would inflict its
lethal click to keep my pocket gopher

from ever getting in, ever penetrating
even one iota of volcanic activity
just beneath the skin—
those outwardly soft surfaces infected
by motherhood and lips.

Graos

"A thousand roads lead...forever to Rome"

Liken me to *Gerontion,*
      still I'm a woman
come to this room with its mauve curtain,
these less than lavish quarters,
my ledger empty.

All around the rented house—
winter-wrapped, dysphoric—
acts I've done to deserve removal
from those other, well-appointed mansions
circle like winds
      from four quarters.

I face into the wind to learn
      the scent
of past misdeeds.

Lost and old, witless
with complaint, I think
of the *Judas* tree. Its likeness poses,
black on white,
      here in *Little Latvia.*

Lija turns into her driveway,
still drives at ninety.
Today I saw her walking back from market,
carrying a single bag.

Will time force me in upon myself
until I turn hard as the yolked egg
      each morning brings?

It must be the rattle trap garage,
tented, dilapidated, falling in upon itself,
that drew me to my wallet,
where I fetched the last check.

Now pots sit askew
        in other pots,
boxes plaster a tiled foyer.

And when I'm taken from this house
(has the landlord remonstrated Mrs. S again?)—
when my husband has his way
        and moves east
to the backwaters
where taut, dry breezes conduct
        white birches,
where the skunk wanders
every alley in a town one street long,
three blocks wide—
they will say *Ah, she never wanted*
to live here, so she stayed among
the Norwegians, the Latvians...

They will speak of me
in my absence as if I were guilty
of the crime of perfection,
the vanity of guilt.

Breathe in the headiness of seasons
bearing change in sewn pockets,
still the old outgrow
        their souls.

Mrs. S, you have done your work,
they will say, when my pills

sit on the bedside table
    in little vials.

To be a tenant of the body
means one's chores are never done.

Nobility

Tonight my father is Caliban, standing below the moon,
cursing its dark side. Raising his fist to redeem,
by virtue of neurological disorder,
imagination's tendencies, rife with coprolalia.

Until I spoke to him, I thought my father rude
as well as dead. In monologue,
we find a way—the fakery melts,
ice turns back to blinding sand.

The island always belonged to those
who could never leave its bib of foam,
ribboned with tentacles and bulbed kelp.
The prisoner's softened, now his master

claims to like the creature curled inside its shell.
One antenna browsing like an eye.
Hermit crabs inhabit the mussel's house
as proof that any hollow can be a home.

A Prospero, this one who paints the sky
so black, the island white, would have no inkling
the moon's an orb, round and willing
to roll around, showing different quarters,

donating a crescent to nuptials, offering
its fourteenth day to pink lichens.
How else does the monster
blunder about with chains and clocks,

staring up in idiotic splendor at swan,
dog star, bull, celestial crab?
This tempting of the fates, pushing bedtime
forward till dawn—

why was day created, unless the hammock,
laced tight, could take the weight
of two sleeping men locked
in a savage embrace.

Spare

The half moon
between winter-black
tree trunks,
an ivory lamp
in Paris
where women dress
in wet linen
on cold nights,
scanty rations
for afternoons
gone dark early.
Or an abundance
of sirens, those
who ensnared
sailors equal only
to the rampant
crime of Friday
evening. How close
to frugal can
we come—what
give up without
borrowing
a cup of sugar
to sweeten the deal?
The mercy comes
in time, thin,
lean, scarce—hardly
measurable
for the way
the moon, our
only source-light,
enters before
dusk, hovers
like a gull
at the horizon
long after dawn.

Bluebells

    Fairy thimbles,
hare bells: up close the humility
of Lilliputians ravishes the mind.

    To call fairies
to a convention on Skomer Island,
the bluebells would be rung. This despite
witches hiding inside hedge rows half-breached
on Scottish fields.

    Dead Man's bells,
if the one caught lavender-handed
receives a sign from relatives
who wish to parse his will. Brother
and sister estranged, sister and sister
no longer able to talk on the phone,
nor lean like lilies into one another.

    Hare-bells.
Oceanside, one wave clamors to shore
and, caught by the dunes, crumples into perfect
tubules, curved and recurved, spiked
like Rumpelstiltskin's shoes.

    Constancy might mean
one thing to a husband, another to a wife.
Like gratitude with its stock photos
and feng shui décor. Must humility
always vie with pleasure? Pleasure
be so strongly scented?

            Bluebells: the folk sign
for death, of which the fairies,
ever reticent, say little. Across the stream
a small warrior loads his cannon.
Steadies his stencil-thin tripod, listens.

            Fires across
Gulliver's carapace stuffed with organ meats,
tongue—all the fine delights of Britain
engorged, lodged in the mountainous
stomach, stuffed with blood pudding.

Walking the Spit

When did she swallow brackish water
as these fingers of cord grass do—
beckoning, swollen green.
When smile and burp up silt
spilling in from the estuary at high tide
to submerge logs of driftwood.

There the sandpiper stood,
strangely human on its tan stand,
calling in five pure tones
to find a mate. She's not sure
she could handle the demise
of back barriers, the wasteland.

What about the past,
its tragedies, its secret sweetmeats
in her mouth at restaurants—
lychee nuts in Montreal,
spare ribs in garlic, black crab
lining the bottom of porcelain.

And though she knows
how the graveyard of shells
came to be—delicacies dropped on purpose
by hawk, gull, and osprey
to break out creature-flesh—
she doubts her strand of 8mm pearls,

the Parisian eye on her bow.
She remembers the part of the story
where characters circle back to point A,
find their childhood, learn again
what it was made of: storm waste,
tidal highs and lows, detritus.

The cameo appearance of a rich relative
who has come on behalf
of the gods, his capacity for kindness
far and above the indifference
of nature, which is, she's
certain, the same as contempt.

The Water Lily

Residue of a past
layered deeply over time present.
Burnt Norton come to water.
Ritual gestures of a sun
too pale to care or cure.

Edge looped over edge,
the pine cone sustains rodents.
The dirt is deeper than we are
and more humble. Doesn't mind
a vine or two

crumpled across its face.
Bitten like a fruit, no longer meant
to name the animals
or count rotten obsessions
of a language

too dark to matter.
This lily is not bloody.
It floats on a ceiling of water,
braided tendrils unencumbered
by false modesty.

If this was the place where Mallarme
first passed the entrance
of the page, then beyond would be
an island inhabited
by Rousseau's sleepy plants.

If Miranda

The magician exists, of course,
if only in her imagination.
She's the one who created him—
a daughter always makes her father
see with one eye. The other?
It's gone white as dawn
in an overcast version of Paradise.
The white of an egg
pulled down beneath the lid.
Blindness frightens her, she tries
to make him see
it's only wiles and guile,
a kind of feminine virtue
known and ignored.
He struts the sand like a bird
too sturdy despite the green toes.
He talks history, of the days
before this day.
Toward evening his apology
grows long as a shawl
of prayers, a foam rope.
She's the one who must
reach farther in, find
the play within the play.
Without her probing
who would know the vagaries
of his latest illness?
Who play the scamp,
the scalawag, that rapscallion
bound to haunt the waterfront?

Salt Marsh

Little by little the corpuscles
fill, swell, expand. Until,
distended and swollen, the hand
can no longer grasp
its own water, its greens.

Memory's sponge-soaked
debris in brackish water.
The fingers reach, wiggle,
invite their own demise.

Saddled by low tide, shells
lie where they were thrown,
broken by osprey and gull.
A blue heron stands one-legged,
as if reckoning.

Spider crabs spill
from rocks to culvert.
The octopus clings to its dream
of orange-tendered black.

Balloon of foliage, sleep spirals,
Medusa-trussed, a spurned
daughter's pregnant shape
want to rescue by turns,
and be rescued.

The fingers fill, empty, feather
another Ophelia's face.
They learn histrionics: to wave,
clap, burnish water's mirror.

The salt marsh harvest mouse,
with cinnamon belly,
travels lightly across driftwood
and sand. Another blind
horizon, then extinction.

A sandpiper calls for a mate:
three pure tones repeated
six times. The man walks
ahead, his form always

falling into the mangrove—
sun reclaiming its last
gold coin: moon at perigee rising
mother-of-pearl swathed
above Protection Island.

Like Little Mouths Drinking From

The fountain—rain and its cousins—
tickling the earth and the girl
who sleeps beneath its crust.

There the geodes lie, eggs unbroken,
with hard shells. Concealment reigns
in the underworld, it makes the girl

and her master thirsty. Not for sweets—
the *rimon* will come, the dog wag
its yellow tail. Like little mouths opening

the lips they've been given, an aural
music. And the cherub astride the fountain,
naked on his horse, his sandals

made as easily from stone as leather.
An urgency inside the bulbs, the roots—
even the Big Leaf Maple whose network

goes deep, limbs branching off
into all the choices made for the girl
by her mother, who gave birth. And the mole

goes on heaping dirt up from the labyrinth,
hands too big for his tiny body.
Sadness in grief too huge for a widow,

the trouble of keeping a girl who disappears
again each autumn as if into the same myth
when finally all the players, who prayed

for this—the ticking metronome
of the waters, rivers filling once again
so their colorless stones might show

a bit of brightness—the same shades
as those worms drawn up from sewers
to lie in the streets of the blessed town.

Notes

Prospero's relationship with Caliban (from *The Tempest*, by Shakespeare) is explored in "Prospero's Lagoon" "Nobility," and "If Miranda". In addition, the poem "Nobility" was inspired by a quote from Coleridge: "Caliban is in some respects a noble being...a man in the sense of the imagination: all the images he uses are drawn from nature, and are highly poetical."

"Such a Long Life" is a line from one of Jack Gilbert's unpublished poems.

"Advancing Colors" refers to any of certain colors (as the yellows and other colors closely related to yellow) that tend to appear nearer to the eye than other pigments lying in the same plane.

In the poem "Grasshoppers," "*ein sof*" refers to "the nameless being" as found in the Kabbalah. The *Zohar* reduces the term to "*ein*" (non-existent), because God so transcends human understanding as to be practically non-existent.

"High-Strung" is dedicated to Lisa Tuininga, who paraglided from Tiger Mountain, Issaquah, Washington, in the summer of 2011.

"Graos" was written after T.S. Eliot's *Gerontion*; it presents a feminine version of his elderly persona.

In "Bluebells," feng shui décor refers to the use of color and harmony in decorating home and offices. This poem is dedicated to Jocelyn Skillman.

"Salt Marsh" was written after a visit to Washington Harbor in Sequim, Washington.

A few poems were written in Cle Elum, Washington, including "Umbel," "Thrum and Goad," and "A Sliver of Heat."

About the Author

Judith Skillman was born in Syracuse, New York, of Canadian parents, and holds dual citizenship. Married to Tom Skillman, she is an amateur violinist, the mother of three grown children, and the "Grammy" of twin girls. She holds a Masters in English Literature from the University of Maryland, and has taught at the University of Phoenix, Richard Hugo House, City University, and the Yellow Wood Academy.

The recipient of an award from the Academy of American Poets for her book *Storm* (Blue Begonia Press), Skillman's also been awarded a King County Arts Commission (KCAC) Publication Prize, Public Arts Grant, and Washington State Arts Commission Writer's Fellowship. Two of her books were finalists for the Washington State Book Award (*Red Town* and *Prisoner of the Swifts*).

Skillman's poems have appeared in *Poetry, FIELD, The Southern Review, The Iowa Review, The Midwest Quarterly, Prairie Schooner, Pontoon*, and many other journals and anthologies. She has been a Writer in Residence at the Centrum Foundation in Port Townsend, Washington, and The Hedgebrook Foundation. At the Center for French Translation in Seneffe, Belgium, she translated the Belgian-French poet Anne-Marie Derèse. Her collaborative translations have appeared in *Northwest Review, BEACONS*, and *Ezra*.

A Jack Straw Writer in 2008 and 2013, Skillman's work has been nominated for Pushcart Prizes, the UK Kit Award, Best of the Web, and is included in *Best Indie Verse of New England.*

Visit www.judithskillman.com

Titles by Judith Skillman

The Phoenix: New & Selected Poems 2007 to 2013, Dream Horse Press, 2014

Broken Lines—The Art and Craft of Poetry, Lummox Press, 2013

The White Cypress, Cervéna Barva Press, 2011

The Never, Dream Horse Press, 2010

Prisoner of the Swifts, Ahadada Books, 2009

Anne Marie Derèse in Translation & The Green Parrot, Ahadada Books, 2008

The Body of Pain, Lily Press, 2007

Heat Lightning: New and Selected Poems 1986 – 2006, Silverfish Review Press, 2006

Coppelia, Certain Digressions, David Robert Books, 2006

Opalescence, David Robert Books, 2005

Latticework, David Robert Books, 2004

Circe's Island, Silverfish Review Press, 2003

Red Town, Silverfish Review Press, 2001

Sweetbrier, Blue Begonia Working Signs Series, 2001

Storm, Blue Begonia Press, 1998

Beethoven and the Birds, Blue Begonia Press, 1996

Worship of the Visible Spectrum, Breitenbush Books, 1988

Glass Lyre Press, LLC
"Exceptional works to replenish the spirit"

Poetry collections
Poetry chapbooks
Select short & flash fiction
Anthologies

Glass Lyre Press is a small independent literary press interested in work which is technically accomplished and distinctive in style, as well as fresh in its approach and treatment. Glass Lyre seeks writers of diverse backgrounds who display mastery over the many areas of contemporary literature: writers with a powerful and dynamic aesthetic, and ability to stir the imagination and engage the emotions and intellect of a wide audience of readers.

The Glass Lyre vision is to connect the world through language and art. We hope to expand the scope of poetry and short fiction for the general reader through exceptionally well-written books, which call forth our deepest emotions and thoughts, delight our senses, challenge our minds, and provide clarity, resonance and insight.

www.GlassLyrePress.com

www.ingramcontent.com/pod-product-compliance
Lightning Source LLC
Chambersburg PA
CBHW020058020526
44112CB00031B/469